Space Weather Report Anthony Nine

Color in the pages for a surprise.

All drawings received automatically from the beyond.

Text channeled by scrying into the art.

Disclaimer: coloring these pages definitely will not attune your neural
pathways to the hidden functioning of otherworld psychic machinery
operating towards an undisclosed purpose, and any dreams you
may receive of star-headed figures in impossible robes
moving switches to change the gears
of a terrible living engine are
purely coincidental.

Space Weather Report © 2019 Anthony Nine | All rights reserved. | Artwork | Writing | Design: Anthony Nine | Reveloit Press. www.reveloit.press | ISBN: 978-1-947544-07-9

Kosí ikú, kosí arun
Kosí ofo, kosí arayé
Fun mi iré owó, iré omó
Iré omá, iré arikú babawá

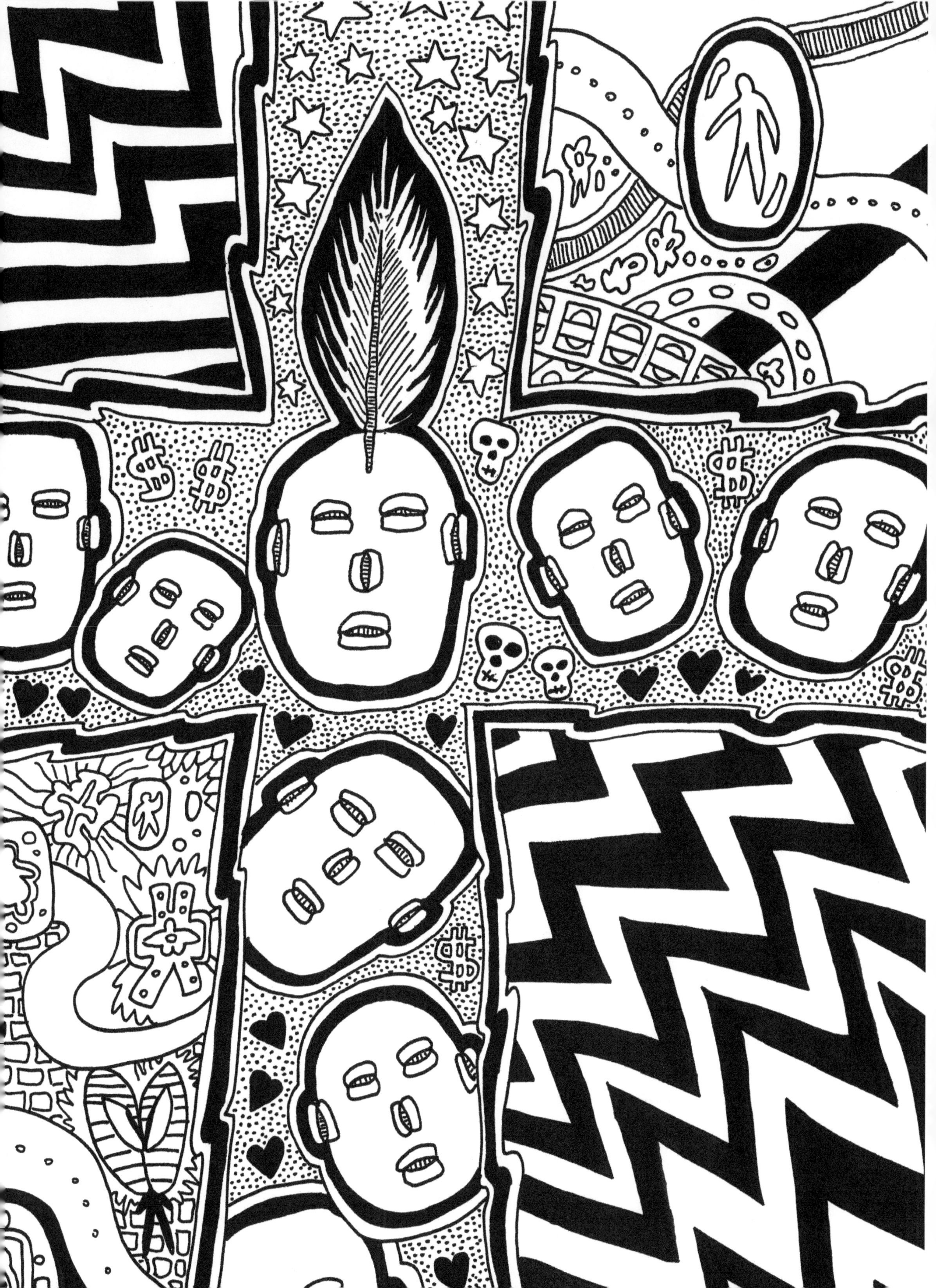

Walking at night. Landscape punk.
City as text. Stray cat and feral fox at the
crossroads at midnight. Dub of London.
Brixton bass pressure. Ghost conversation.

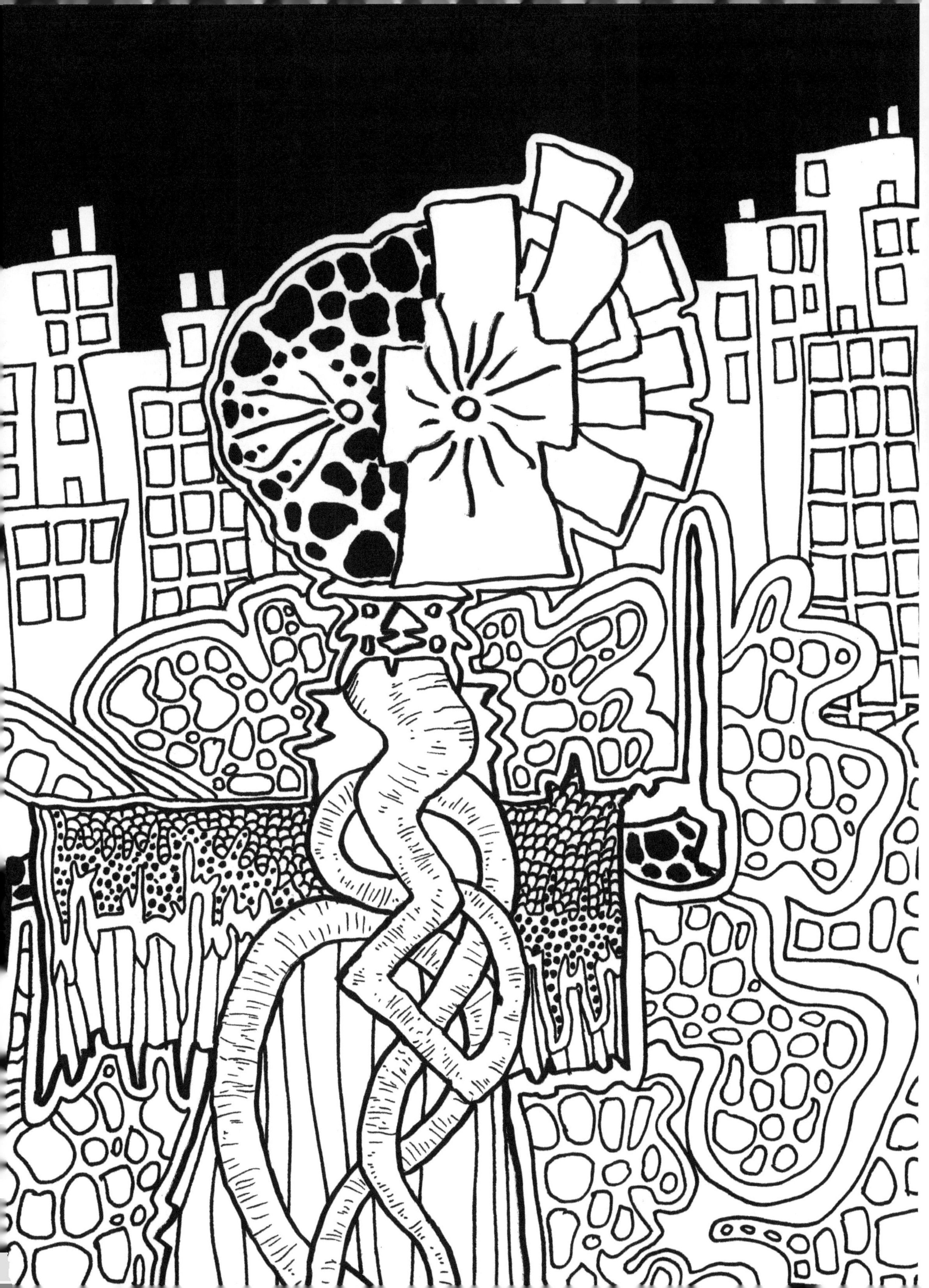

Wet the beak of the princes of the city at the foot of the domino table. London clay is made of people. Smog of life. Smog of my smog. What I see is an intersection of them. A shadow pressed into time and experienced as something easier to process and assimilate.

Midnight sorcerer. Blood pacts and hard exits. Infernal intelligences composed from leaked fragments of human and animal. A weaving of bone and tree. Knitting together and cloaked in a cowl. Mind the doors. Mind the doors.

Smog lust of the city dead. Compass and set square. Masonic circuits and chartered streets. The domino table. Ghost life of sick buildings. Brick upon brick, soul upon soul.

Creature of clay. Mud of my city. Toad of the river. Crowned mariner below the bridge. Decomposing revenants sloshing together in a soup of spirit. Thick and glutinous and sun-starved.

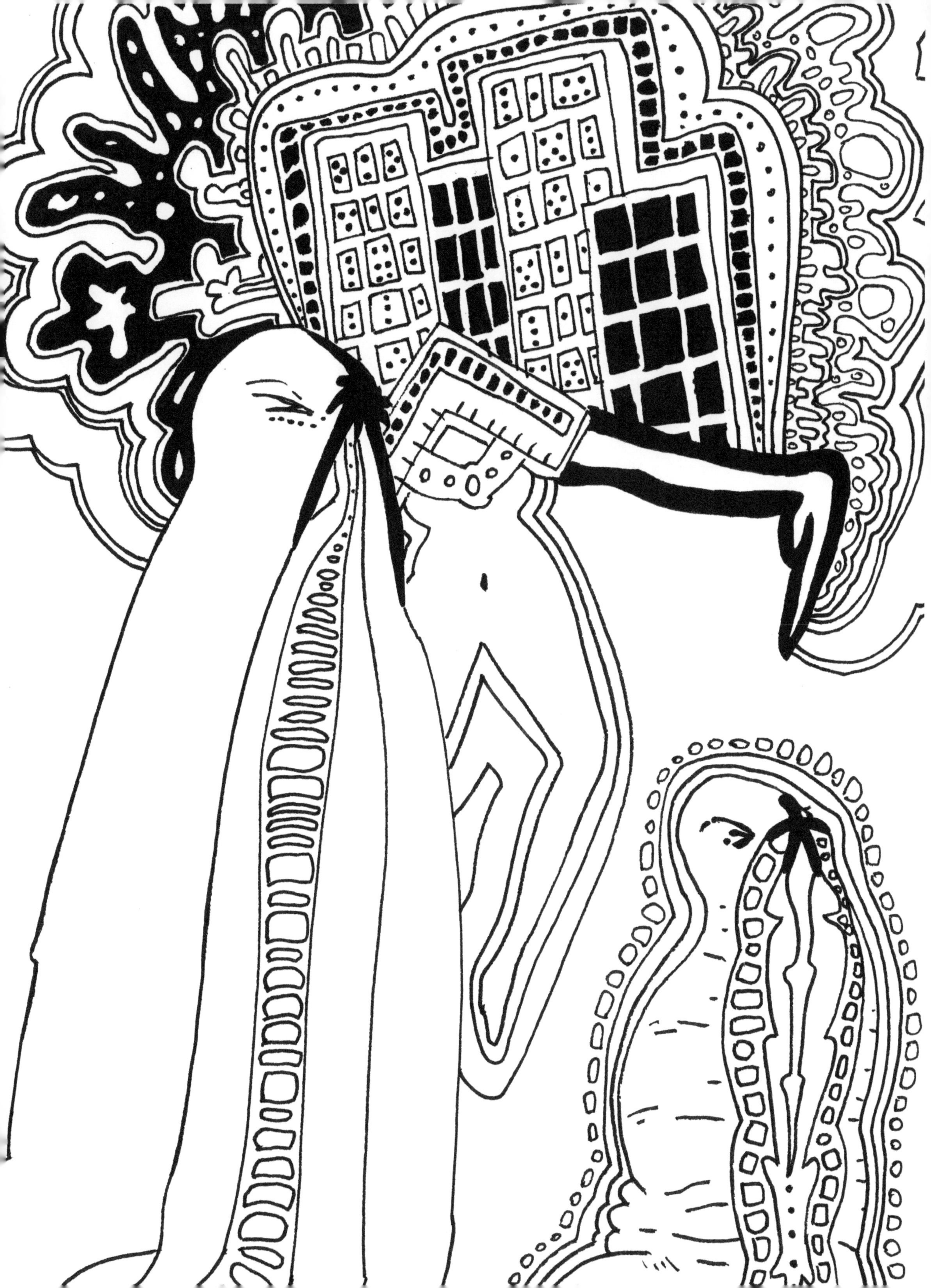

The red-suited professors fed me a poison that placed me through the membrane. I could still see their spirit staffs on the reverse side, surmounted by birds and crowned with the heavens.

I looked down upon the building from above. A gilded citadel of porcelain and gold. Walls like fine bone china beset with gleaming unnameable devices.

The black house rose in the distance. Turrets visible over the battlements. Shadow upon the land.

Four presences dressed as the elements gather about a Snakes & Ladders board without any ladders.

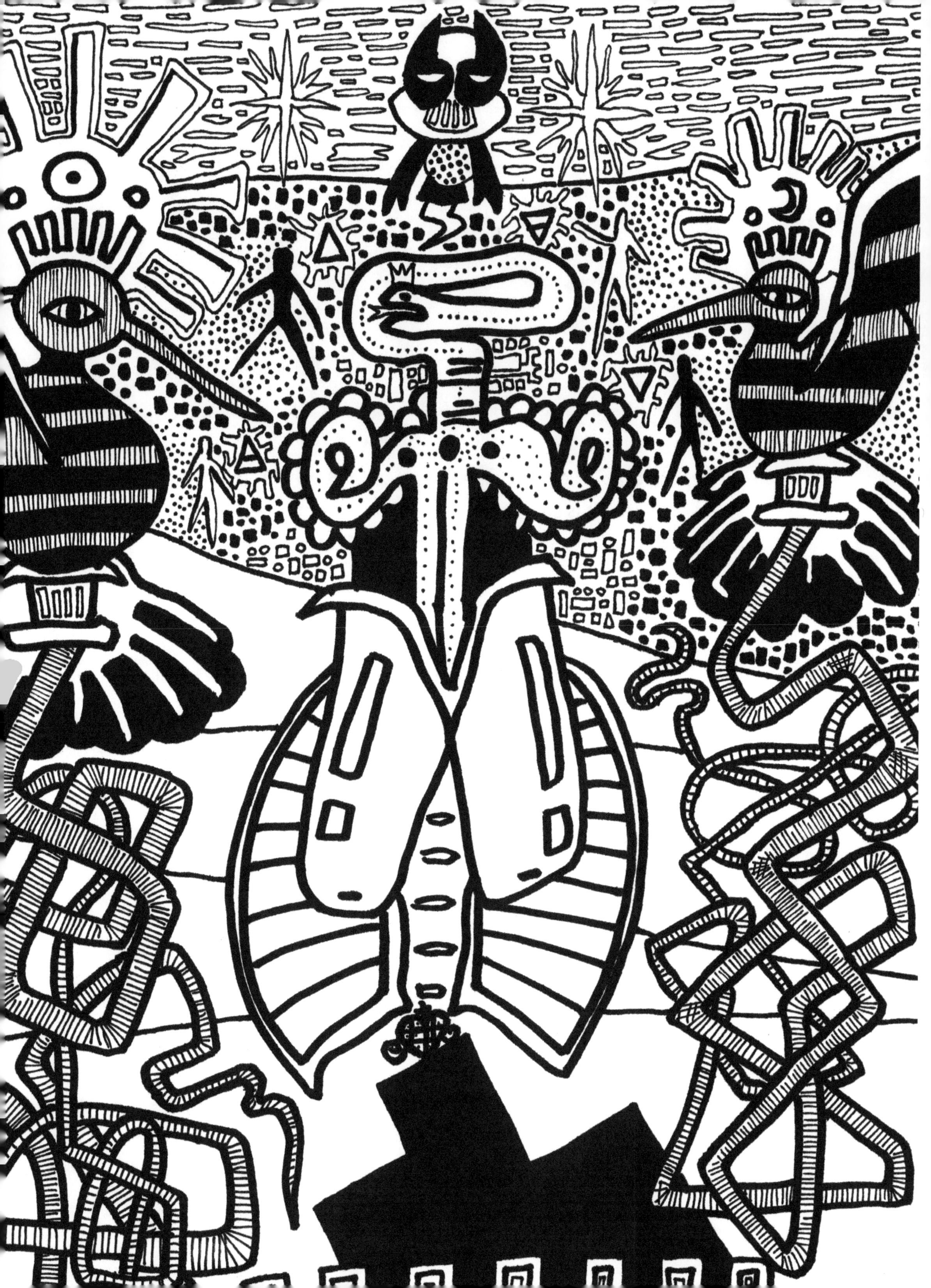

Repetition of the practice helps to cultivate the body of
spirit. When it is sufficiently developed, the star begins to
form with its attendant spirits and the vision can then erupt.

The sight gives witness to crooked road and black lane.
Enveloped within this form and with fresh eyes one can
traverse the territories and become familiar with the local
politics and flora.

Wild Thicket, Blood Root, Liquid Skeletons,
The Hum, Nine Red Rosebushes, The Bathhouse
and Soiled Trinovantum.

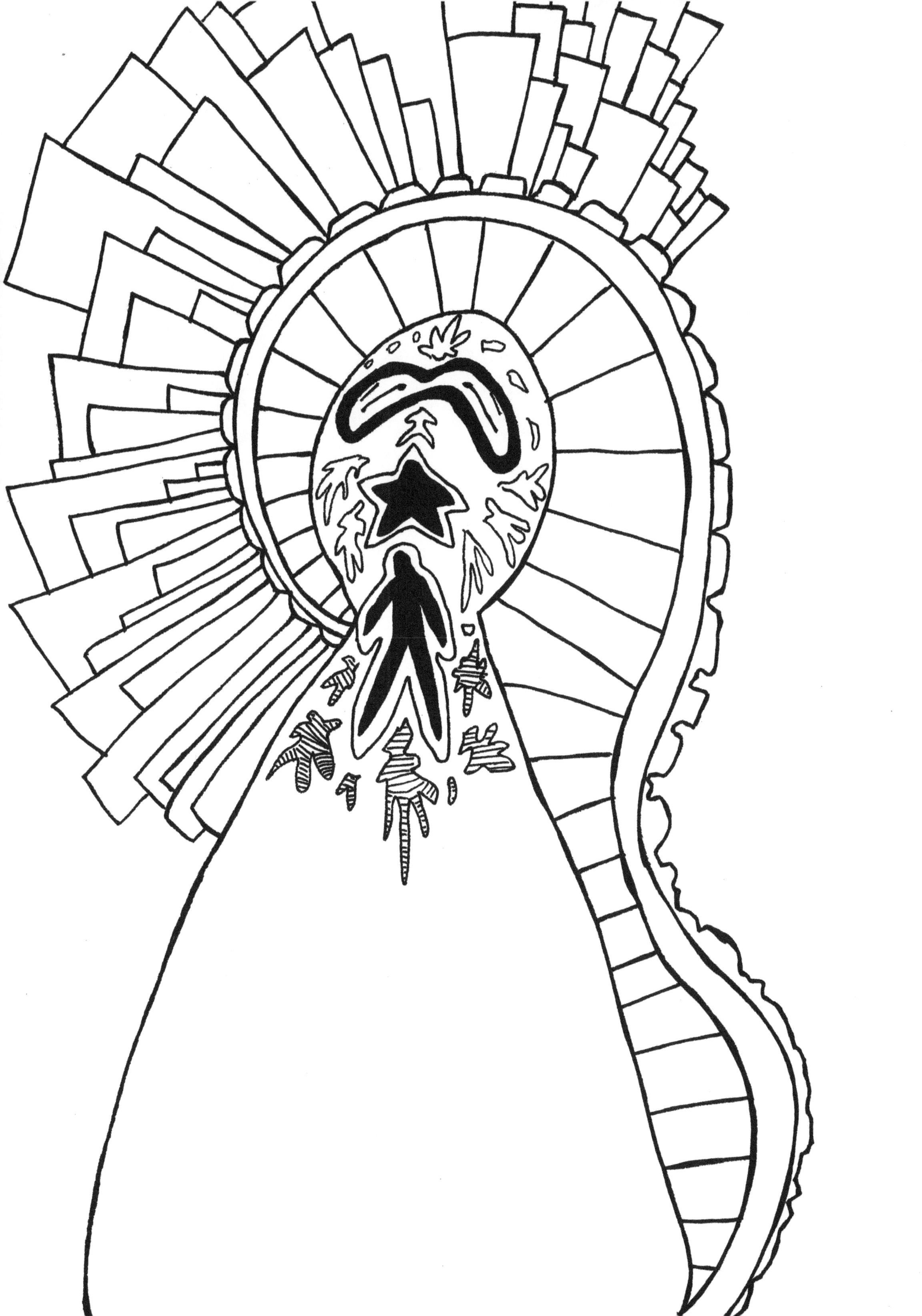

It can be unsettling when the sight is stirred. Persistence
is required to cultivate a sense of poise within the onrush
of new sensory impressions and fluctuating stairways
floating amid liquid effluvia.

In time it becomes apparent that several rhythms are
in play and certain processes of its organic function
can be intuited. Within the shifting terrain it is possible
to observe fixed locations and starry eruptions or
disturbances throughout its expanse.

It is not uncommon to see other personages moving with
purpose within its fold, and the cultivated body of spirit
can make it difficult to discern if the travelers are humans
possessing the sight or the denizens of elsewhere.

Swarms of predatory birds inhabit the less explored
reaches but the fluids required to enter and navigate
these regions is sufficient deterrent much of the time.
A silver coin can be given to the Mariner for steerage and
swiftness upon these waters.

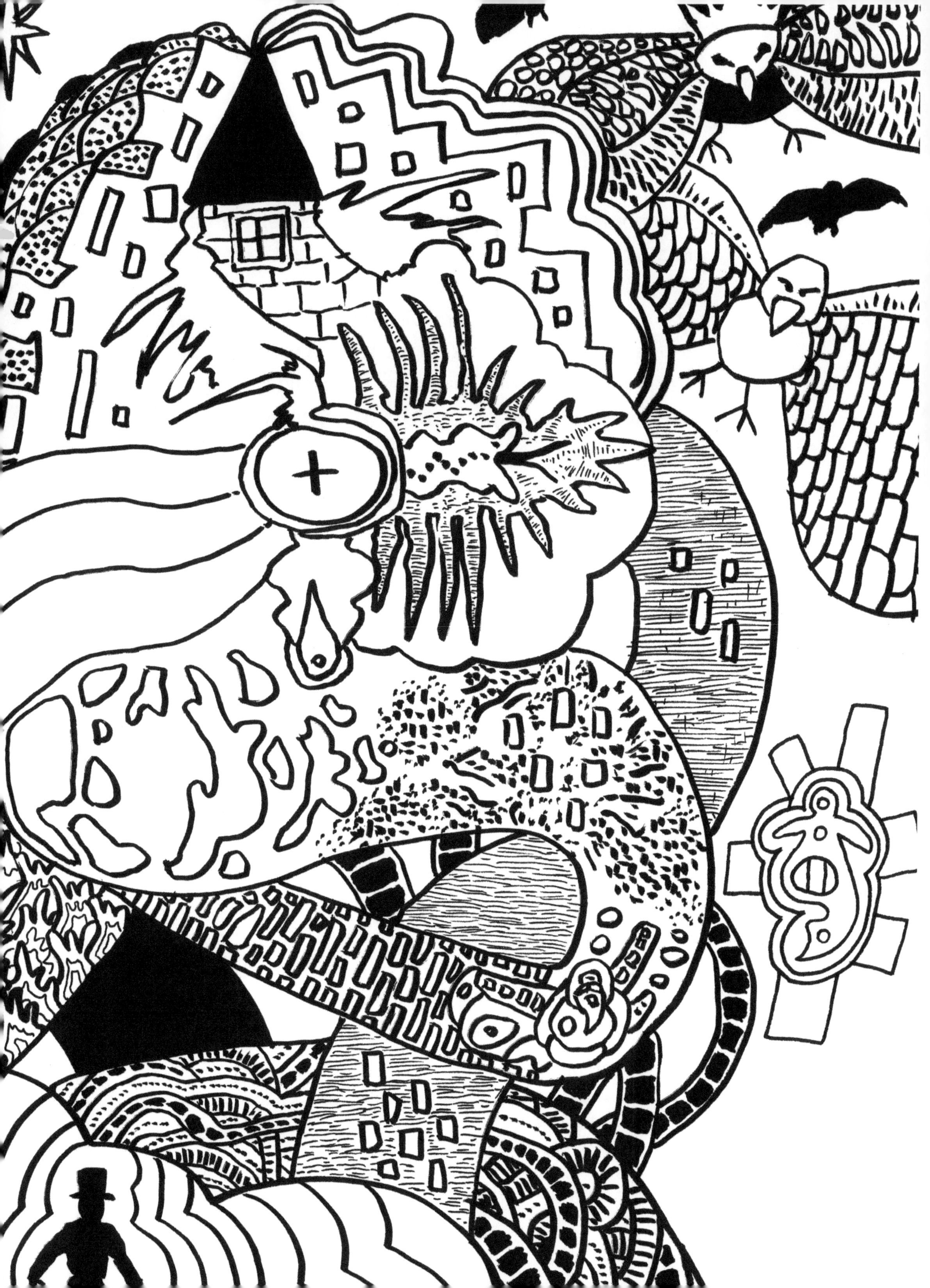

At the moment of ingress, ones own fragment of laterite will cast a stone today and make a door yesterday. From the vantage point of the crossroads, you can peer back to the roots. Your own ancestral cord winding back through time, and entangled with the physical site itself. A pathway made of the footsteps that trod this intersection, and your every transaction here winds your own cord deeper around the roots of this place.

A necessary orientation must occur as you become cognizant of the presences that congregate about your territory of the tree. Hot access to lush channels of mystery. The life-giving serpent and the ruling archangel. Presences that you are bound to in old family pacts, waiting on the other side to take account. Satellite spirits that are in sympathy with your nature. Bestowing an inflammation of the seventh sight or putting the heart stick in your open palm. A root or branch or line, sometimes given as a literal stick.

Clear sight may be cultivated of the roads and pathways that are open. Doors that can be tried and invisible houses between the houses on the invisible street. Sometimes you can find a keyhole for a key that has been lost, but the location of the door is still known. Faculties that can be sought. Creaking gates that may be prized open. Skeleton keys that can bid rusted-shut doors to unlock.

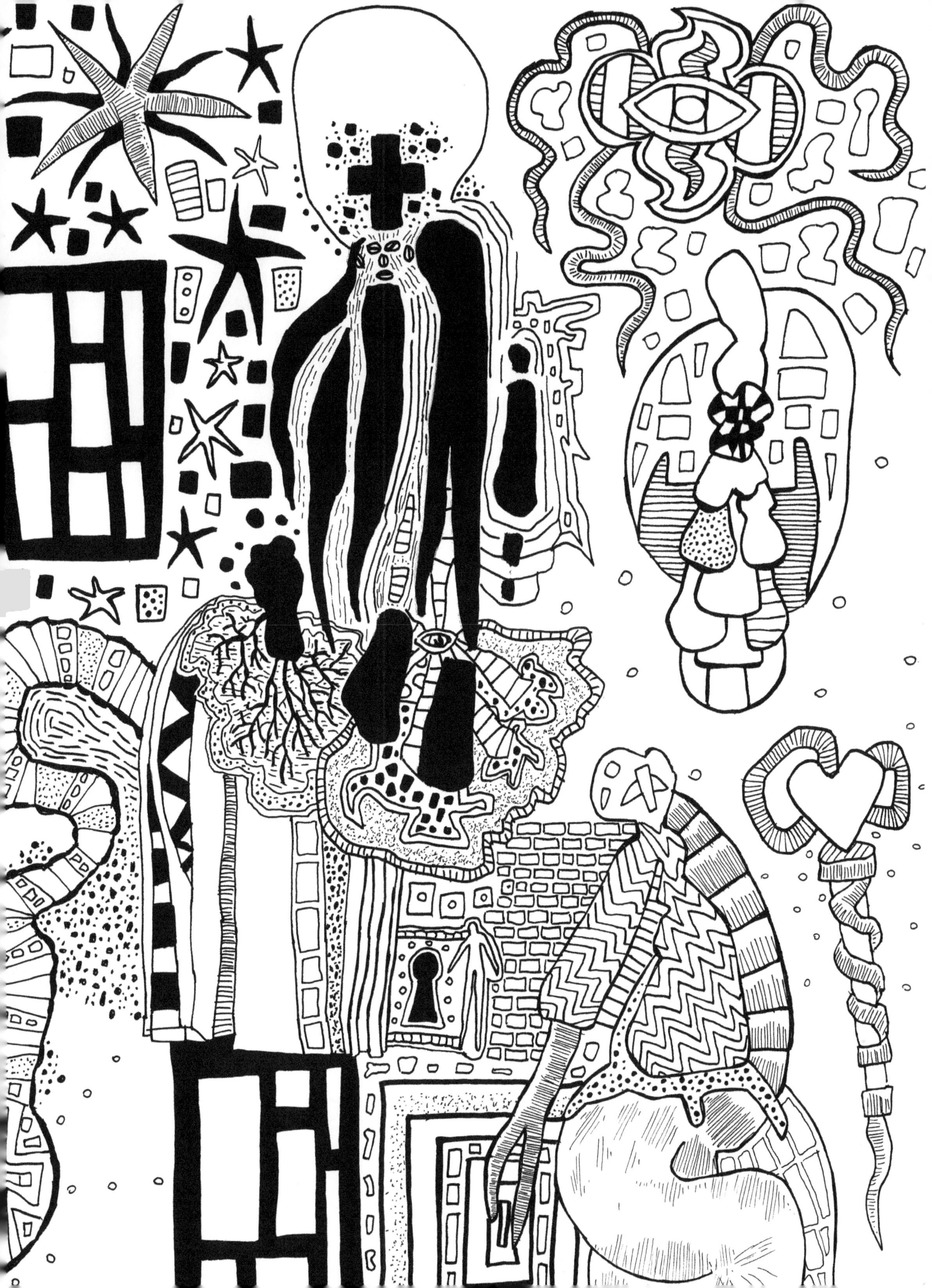

Starry immersion causes the development of one's body of spirit. Heart aflame and crowned with the sovereignty of the winged. Successive layers of ectoplasmic substance warding off predatory glimpse spores and simple parasites. Tough enough to pulse back solid under the churn and raging texture. Triumphant and impossible hawk like tearing beak and rending claws. A feather in the wing of the soaring falcon. Arising in opulence and drunken jewellery on the tearing limb from limb.

You can see the staff of spirit from here in its fullness. Complex layers of dead folded upon one another amid shifting humours. A constellation of stars swarm like glorious moths about the substance of your Egun. Lancet pierces the bark and blood at the root seeps into salivating mud. Burning embers in the dirt like the antiseptic apparition exalted. Assisting in the repair and resurrection of scorched limb and stunted waste.

Behind you is the crossroads and the arrangements that you have made there. Always located at your foundation and present for counsel. About you circle the full orbit. Flash of spirit. Blazing fire. Seven bolts of lightning. Seven strong ceiba. Visceral sack cloth and the broom that sweeps out. Crowned king of the earth. South London spirits in my bag. Hazel wand in the hour of Mercury. Snake in the grass. Drip of fang. Circumstance of the moon on the sweet election.

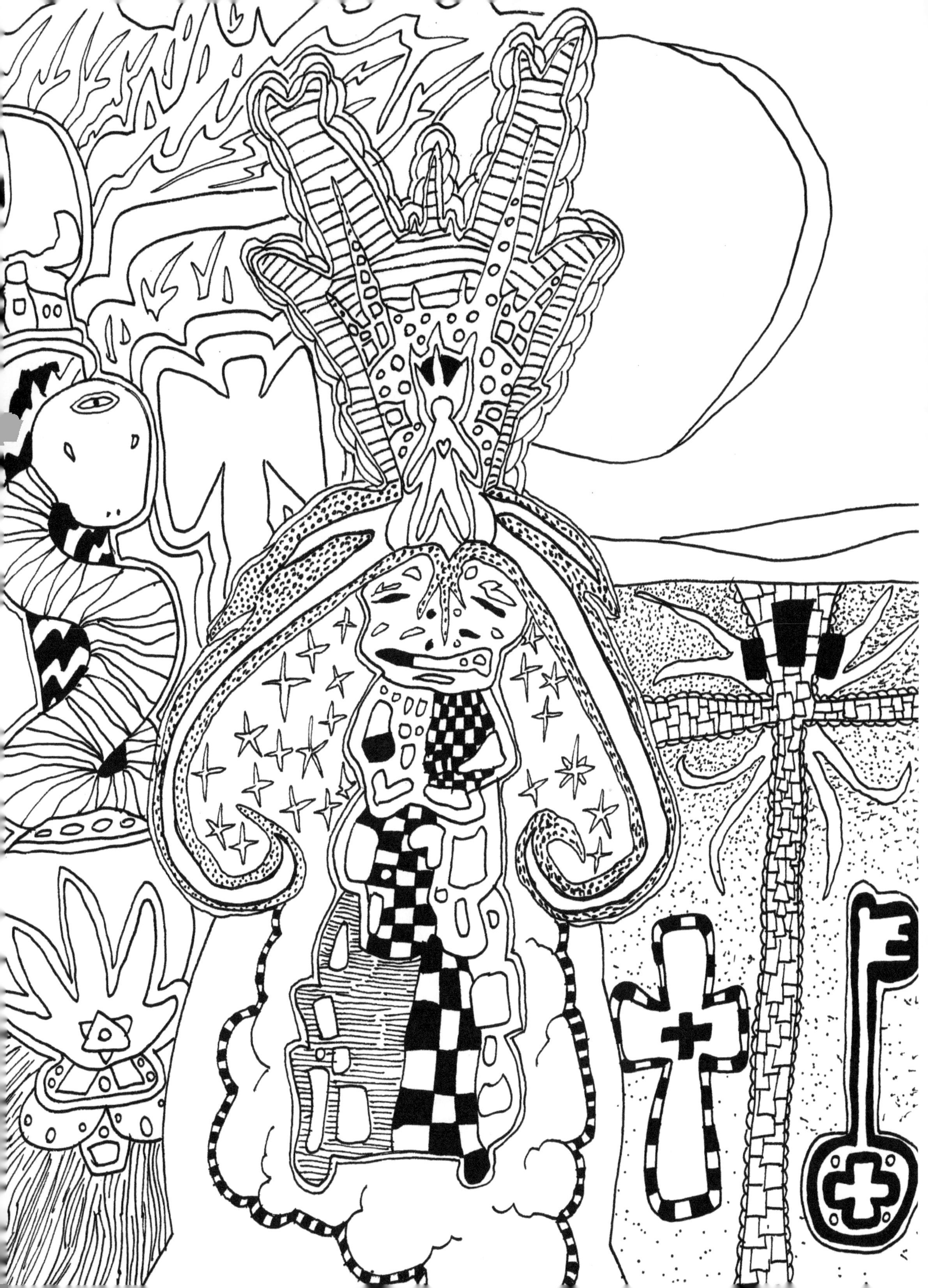

Mirage of ghost sediment. Salivating mud.
Soil of the dead. Shifting sands form a
pattern for scrying. The four pulsating hearts
in space. Red viscous liquid coursing through
vast tubes and pipes. Invisible machinery
within a communion wafer. Sublunar sound
and the buried heart.

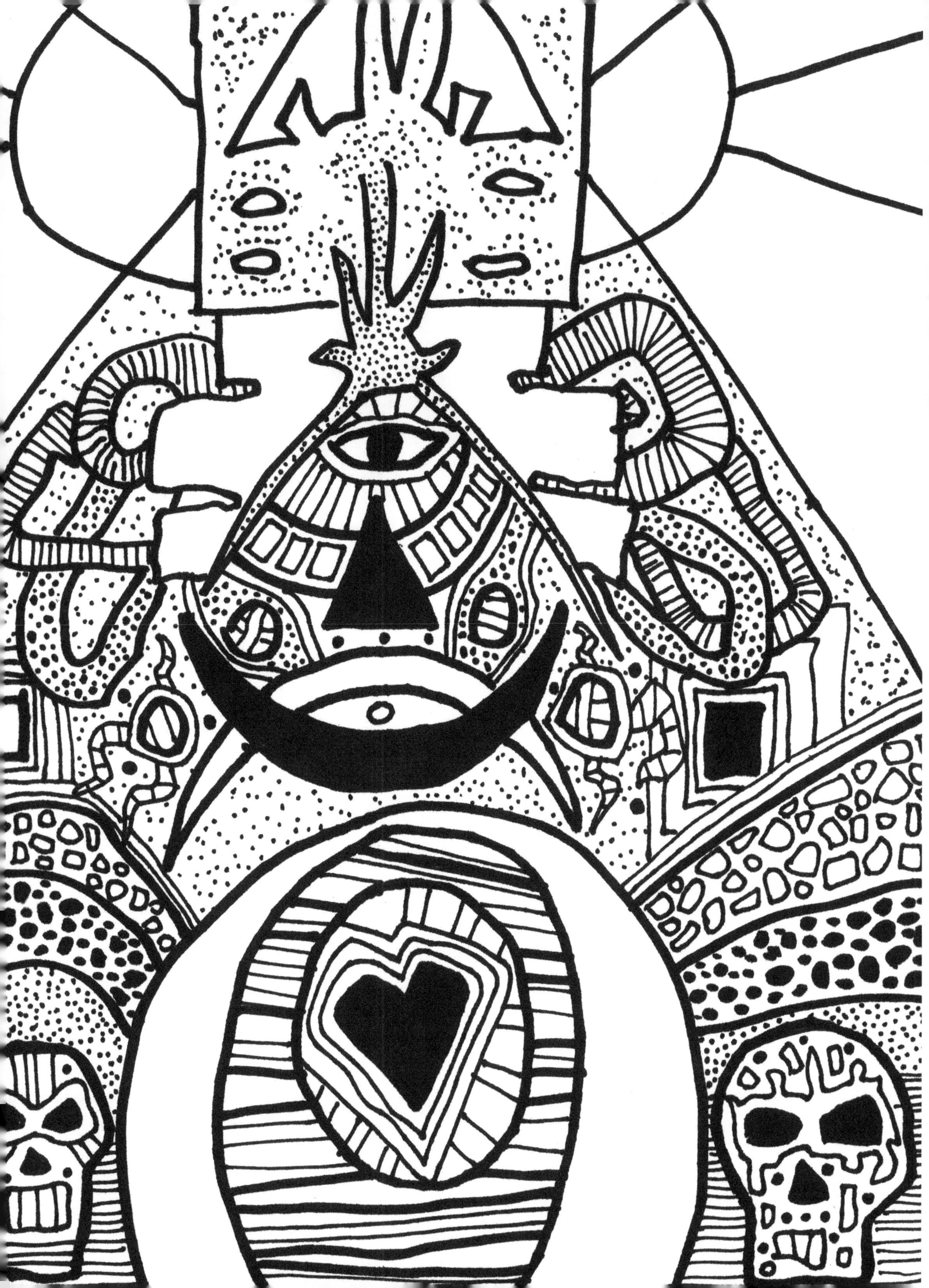

Around the domino table the tokens of our fate unfold.
Tears that have fallen heavily are embedded in the
structure of this place.

The machinery sends out a great limb made of celestial
pipes or tubing, and a plethora of liquids melt and solidify
into a composite shape. Texture breathing through
porous membranes.

A figure is drawn towards it out of the void, features
indistinct, a humanoid shape bathed in light with three
whirling vortices at its centers.

A pulsing organ erupts from the tip of the pipe and quickly
grows under the heat and light of its sun. Below are the
chthonic vibrations and the slow pulse of the dead. The
crowned serpent and the lush garden.

Three observers look in on this scene from the other side of
the machine. I speculate on whether I appear the same to
them, as a disembodied eye peering in from another place.

The scattered dominoes begin to organize themselves
into an augury above the flourishing heart fruit. The three
observers understand and their eyes alternately show
tears, mirth and revulsion at the cast figure.

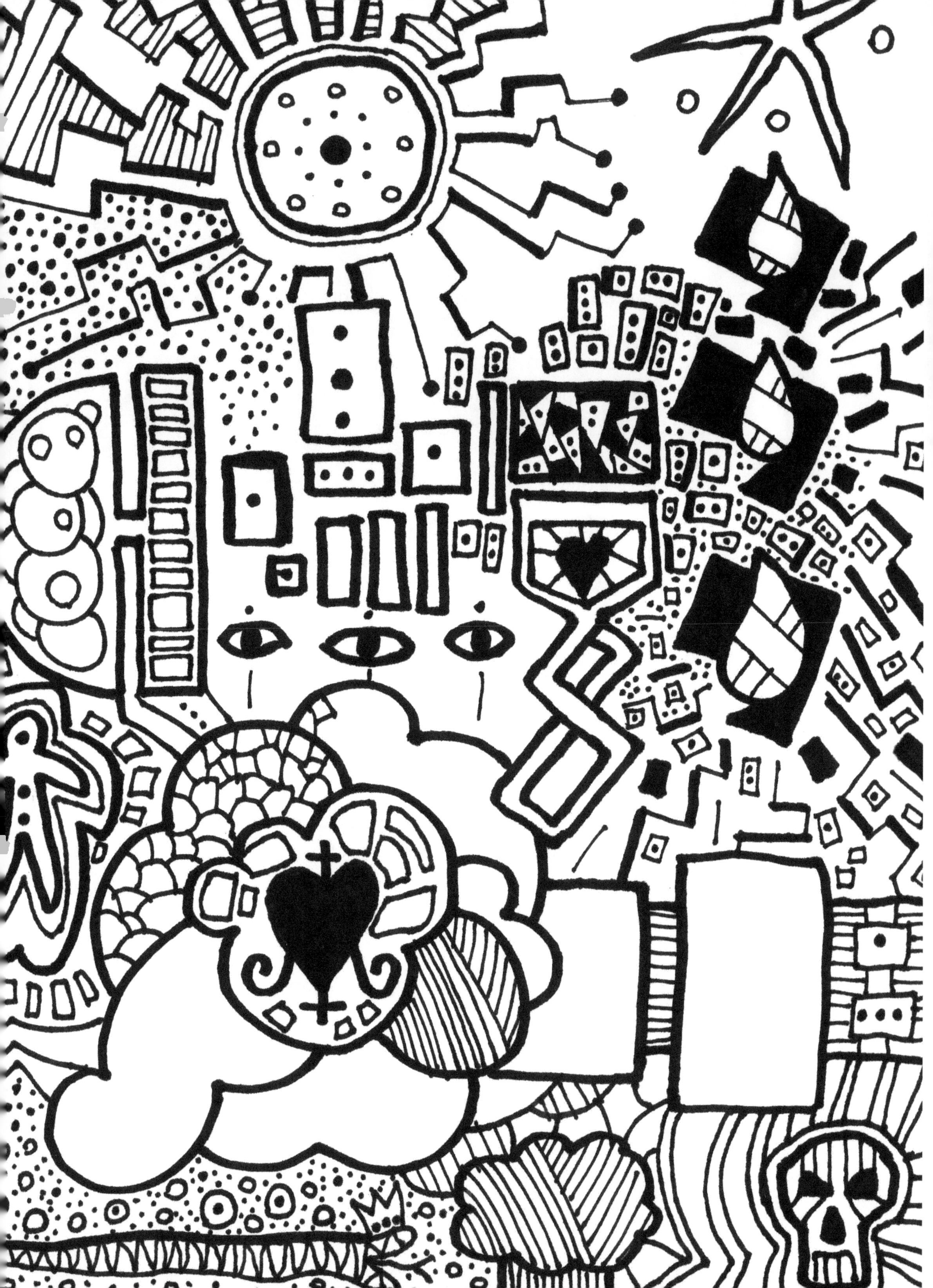

Three figures come forth within moments of passing through the next membrane. The first offers something to me from a tray, or invites me to operate a control panel. It is propelled upon large interlocking spheres like flower petals, and it is unclear where the being ends and its headgear begins.

The second visitor stepped to me with a jab of memory. It was as if I had one of these as a child, but that couldn't be right. Something that I had found on the floor and thought was a bug but it wasn't. I kept it with the rest of my toys and it would come into my dreams at night. Then it was gone and I had never thought of it again until.

The third approached as a mass of pipes and chimneys. Steaming forward on great pistons. Circumference of gigantic churning banks and its visage an unconvincing jovial mask, as if it were an idea plucked from my head of what it thought I would want to see. Rasping robot voice and the face of a leering cloud.

Behind them either a great serpent or a doorway.

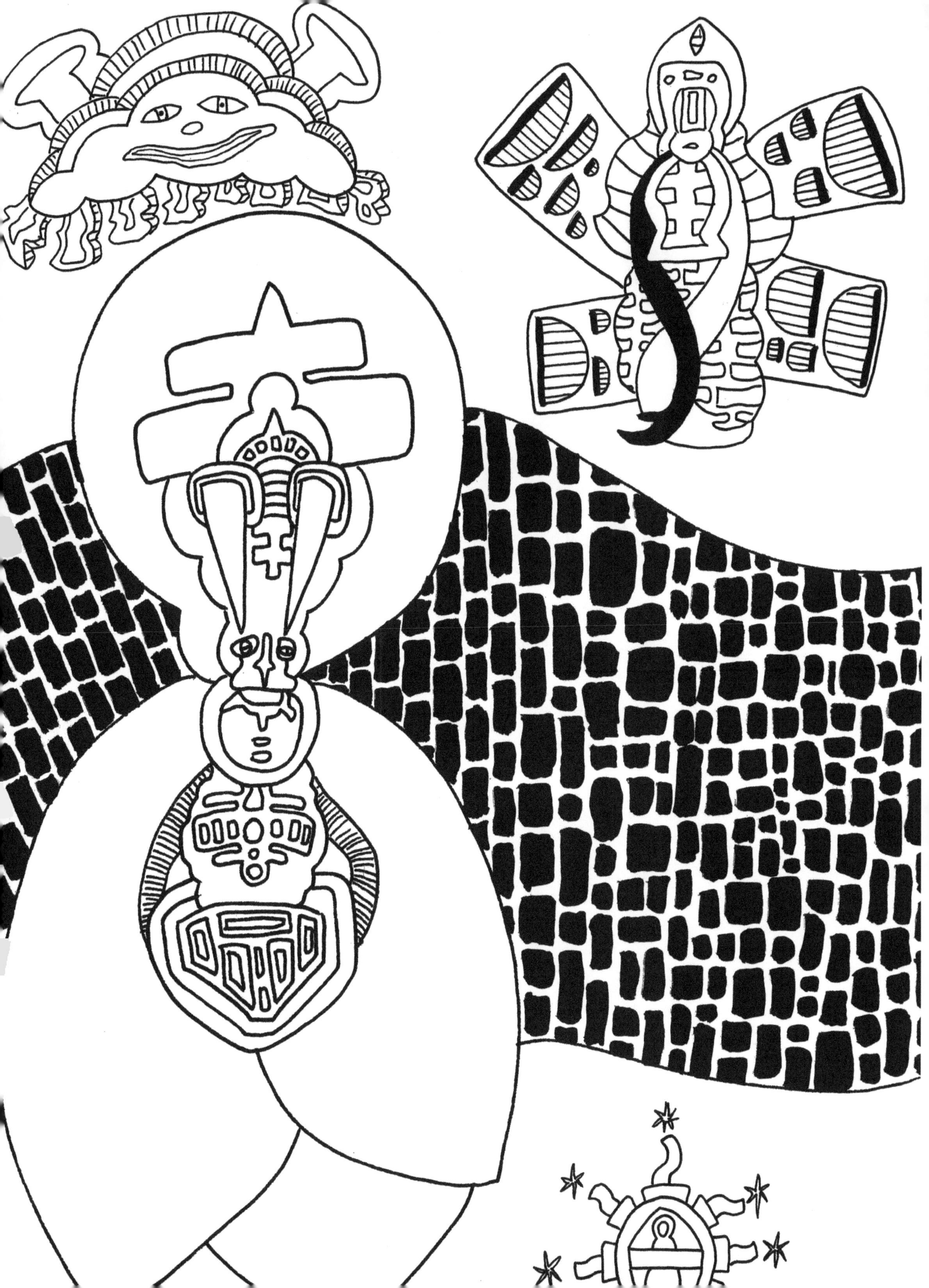

Don't think about cats. The ring encloses my circumference. A magic circle nine feet across. Perfected as the Golden Mean. Sudden glitch reveals my true body. Miraculous serpent coiling in time. Look through the glass window to where my heart incubates. A botanical garden of longing. Awake and propelling itself on awkward wings somehow perfectly suited to the unique terrain. Dark clouds stare daggers as we silently drift by. Four faces see but must not be seen.

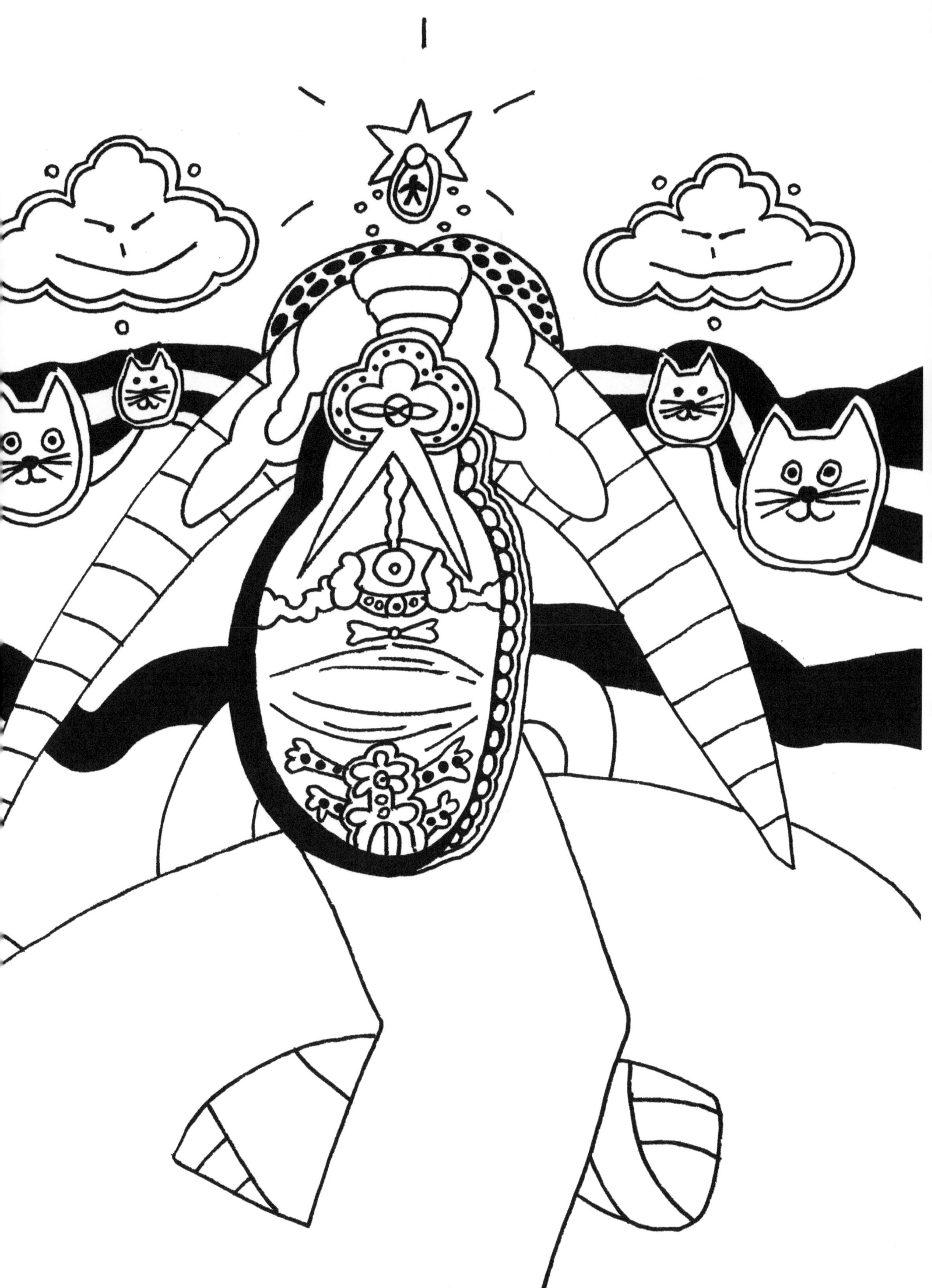

The Mountain is one of several fixed points within
the shifting terrain. A reliable course can be plotted
by reference to its landmark. The lore implies that its
presence reflects the spirit life of a physical mountain
located in remotest Antarctica. All mountains are
understood to have a degree of sentience, difficult to
fathom on the physical plane, but observable here where
its true character is evident.

The mountain displays a certain malignancy. Its demeanour
is that of an alien parasite lodged within a landscape it
has invaded and hurriedly engaged in an activity that
resembles mining. Although there are manuscript records
that reveal the mountain has been here for centuries, there
is a palpable sense of urgency to its active work, as if it is
expecting to be caught red-handed at any moment.

Other presences swarm about the mountain. Creeping Beak
acts as an emissary or ambassador. Projecting itself through
star tunnels to be the eyes and ears of the mountain within
the terrain. Cloud Worm acts as interpreter. Relaying
messages back and forth for its employer. It is never certain
if these entities have been pressed into its service or are
acting opportunistically of their own volition and prospering
within its eco-system. Sometimes other figures can be
glimpsed operating within the workings of the mountain,
enslaved or assimilated to its will.

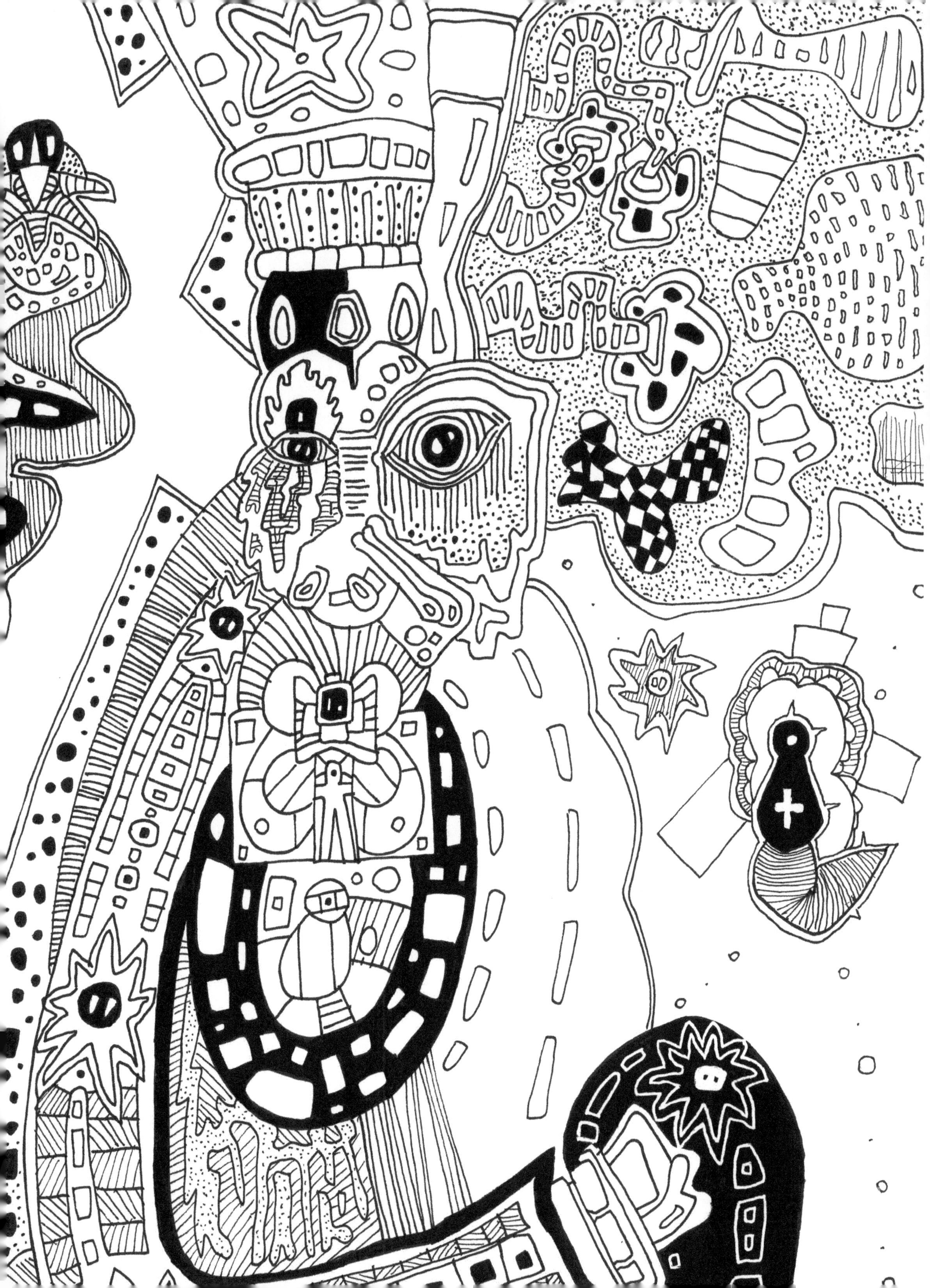

Don't ask any questions. Just get in the car. The Backwater is a humid wetland within the ambience of the Westway Angel. The brackish waters of its canal networks are frequently visited by those who wish to establish a pact or broker an introduction. A melancholy humour permeates the waterways and can pull down those susceptible to its allure.

You may encounter those who wish to share with you a map, and much discernment should be made before choosing to step into a car and close the door.

Inhabitants of the Backwater are few, yet regular presences frequent its byways and ply their trade. Turtle Mary, Hopping Jack and Love's Parade.

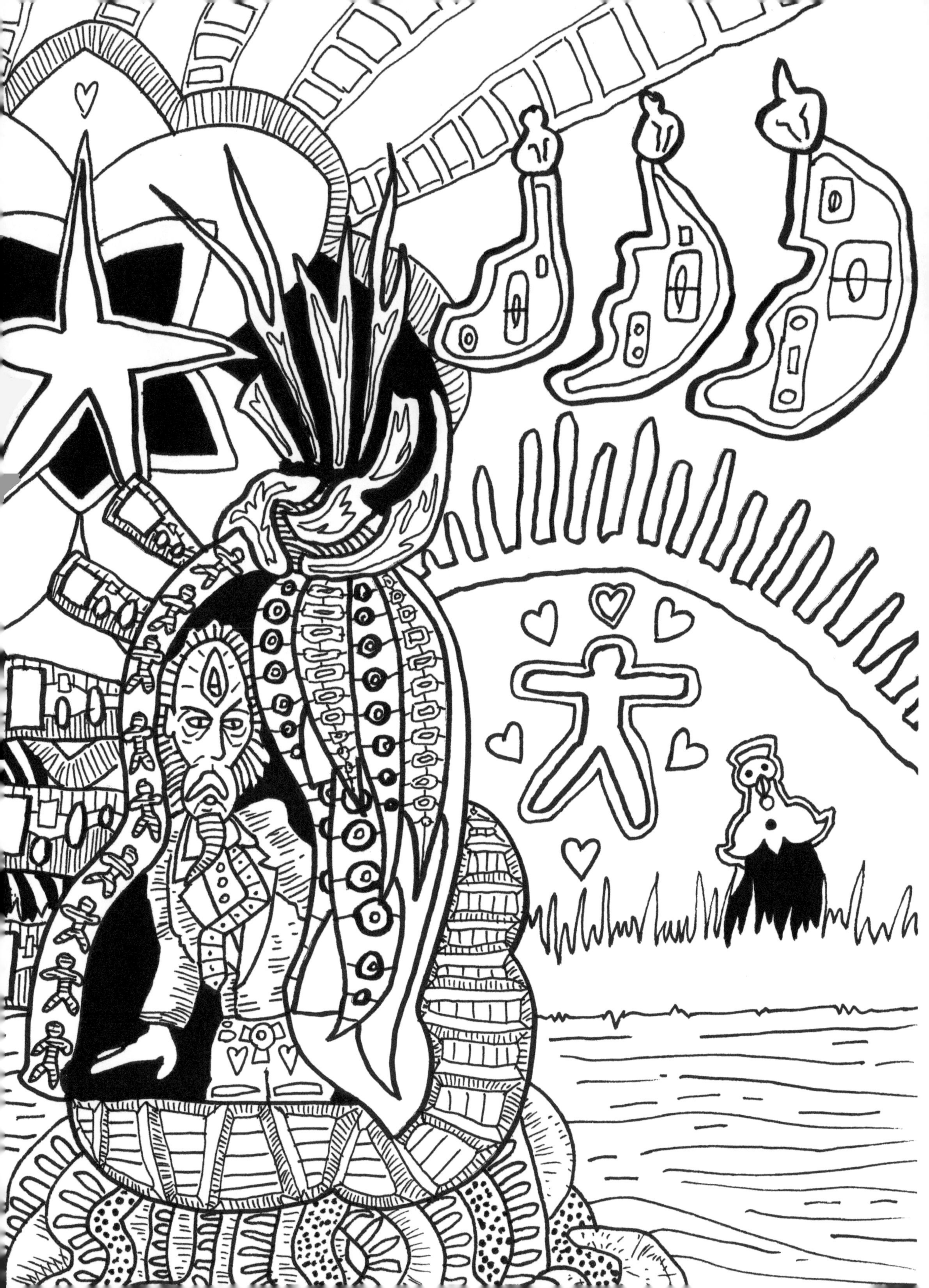

Pavel Mikoyan is Screaming On the Moon. The court of cats traveled for a century to witness the burial of the cadaver. Do not remove the cosmonauts bones. A seed planted in Moon soil. Tropical alien vegetation sprouts from the vivified remains.

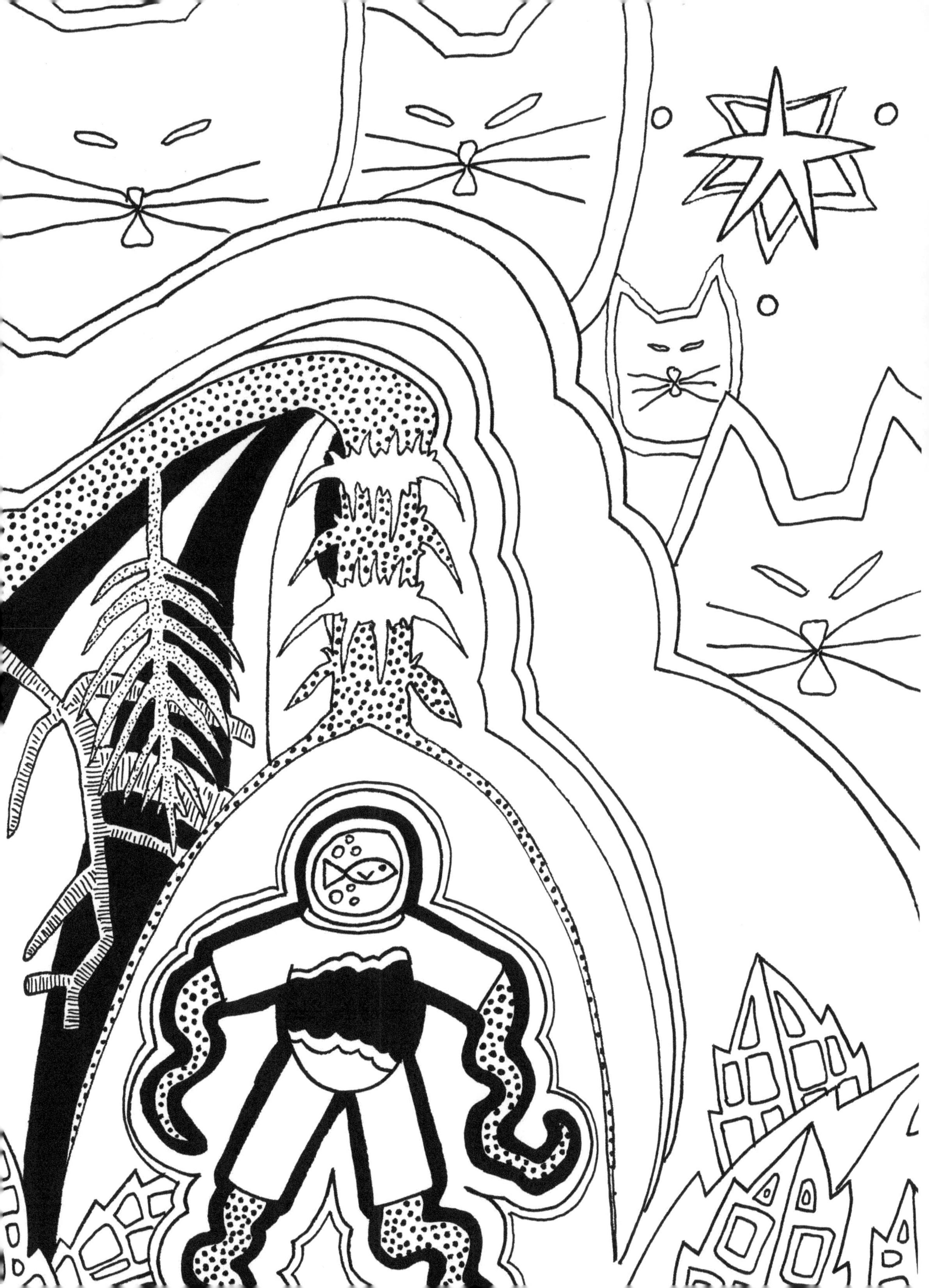

The king that rules in this frequency is crowned with
Solomon's house. Flanked by Kid Horus and Cardinal
Domino. Body formed of the gears and processes of
this place. Juice of its radiance nourishing the body of
spirit. Instructing in the knowledge of things natural and
celestial. Letters cut into spirit with invisible burin.

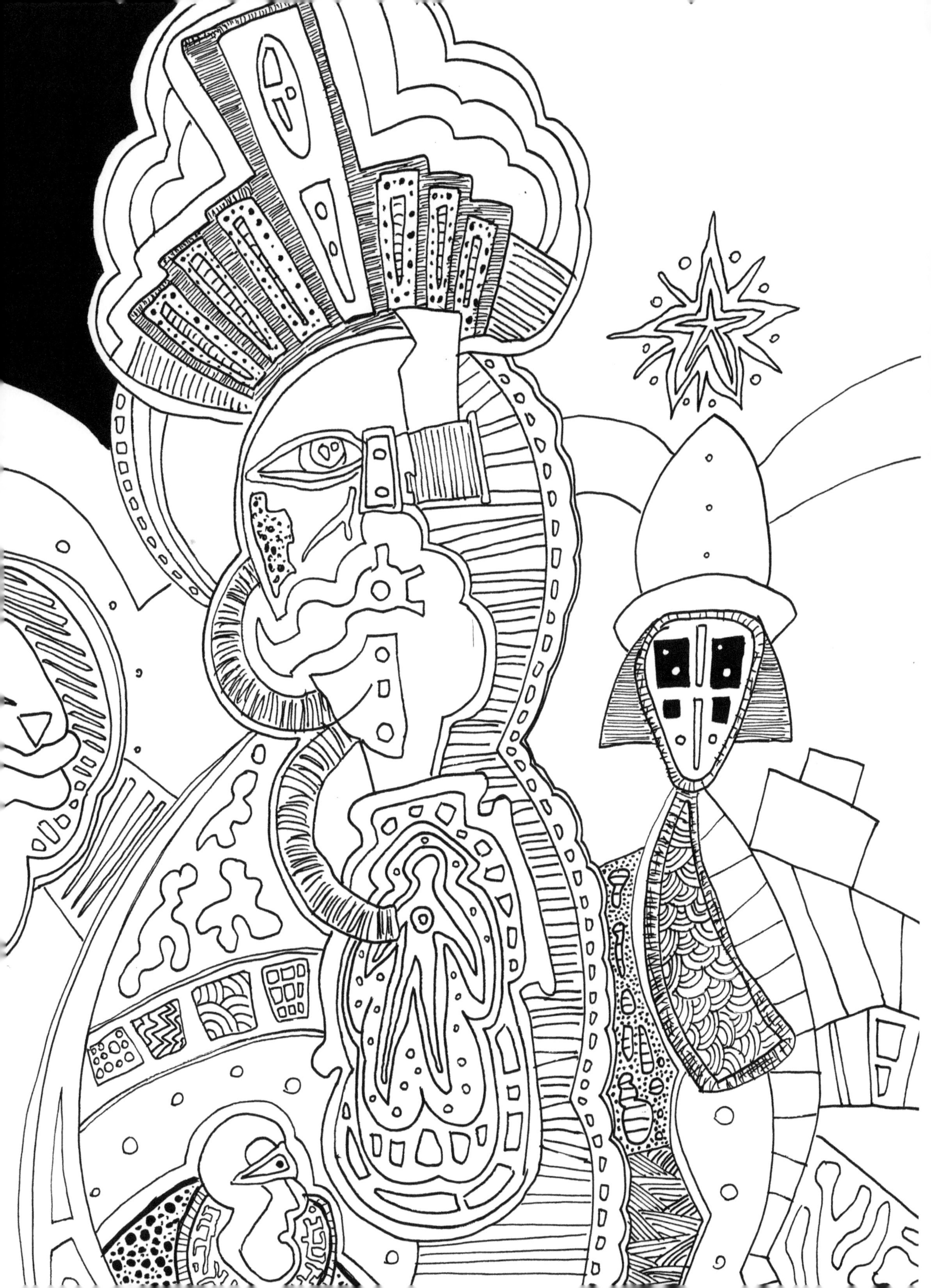

Delfonic tunnels beckon and you tumble. Free-floating in an immaculate white suit through a sensuous terrain of ambient colors and soothing orchestral soul music, while beautifully manicured hands appear from the ether to pass you ludicrous cocktails at just the right moment. The camera fades to soft focus as the bedroom door closes.

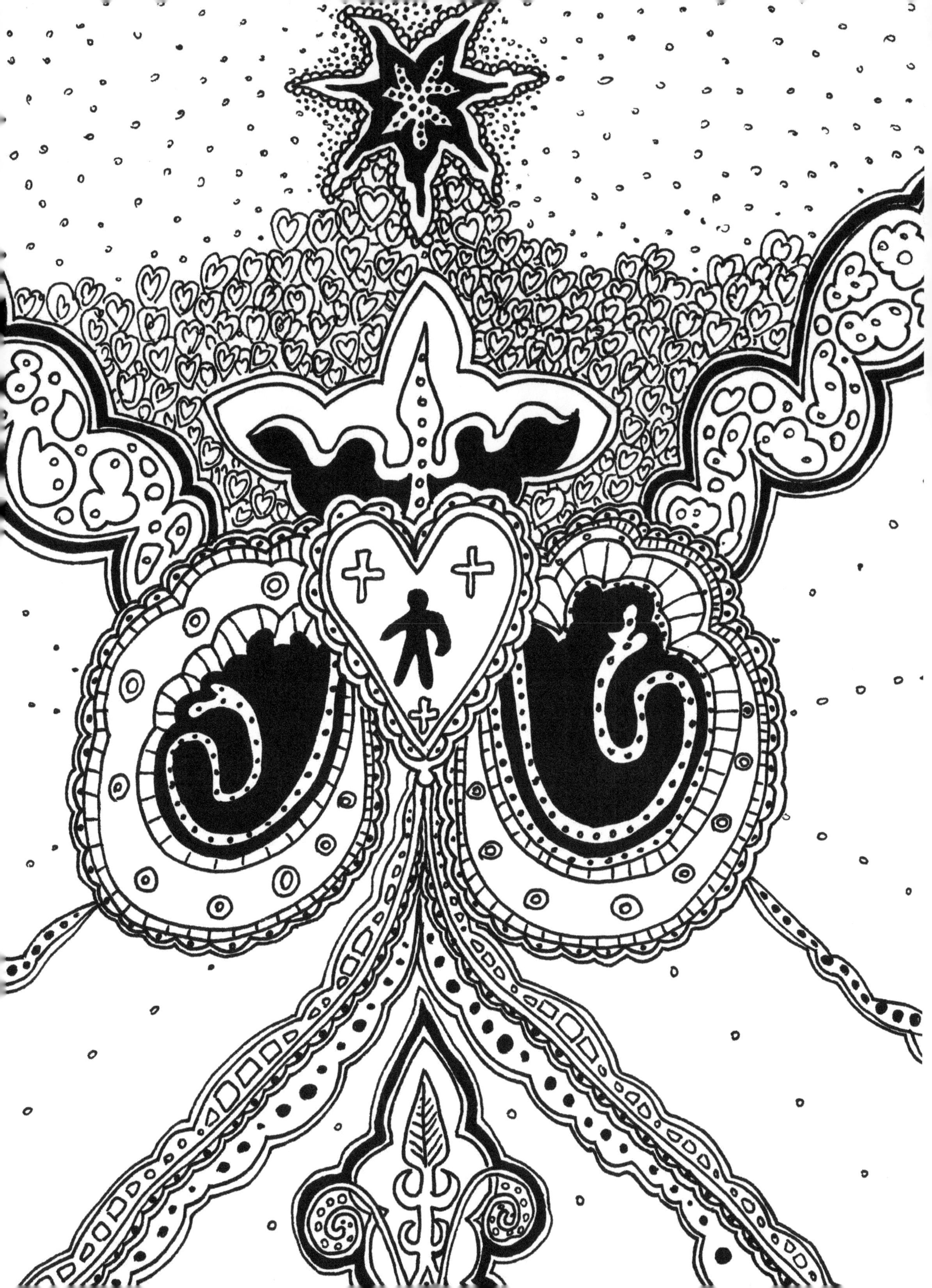

Alive below flicker of screen and billboard scream moves
the forgotten. A rapture of the senses in the colors of
earth. Storehouse of medicine and cabinet of poisons.
Thick woods dense with secrets. Dirt, wood, leaf, flower,
fruit, root and water subject to celestial tide and starry
conflagration. The process of growth within time. Wizened
door opens for blood cut to the original pact.

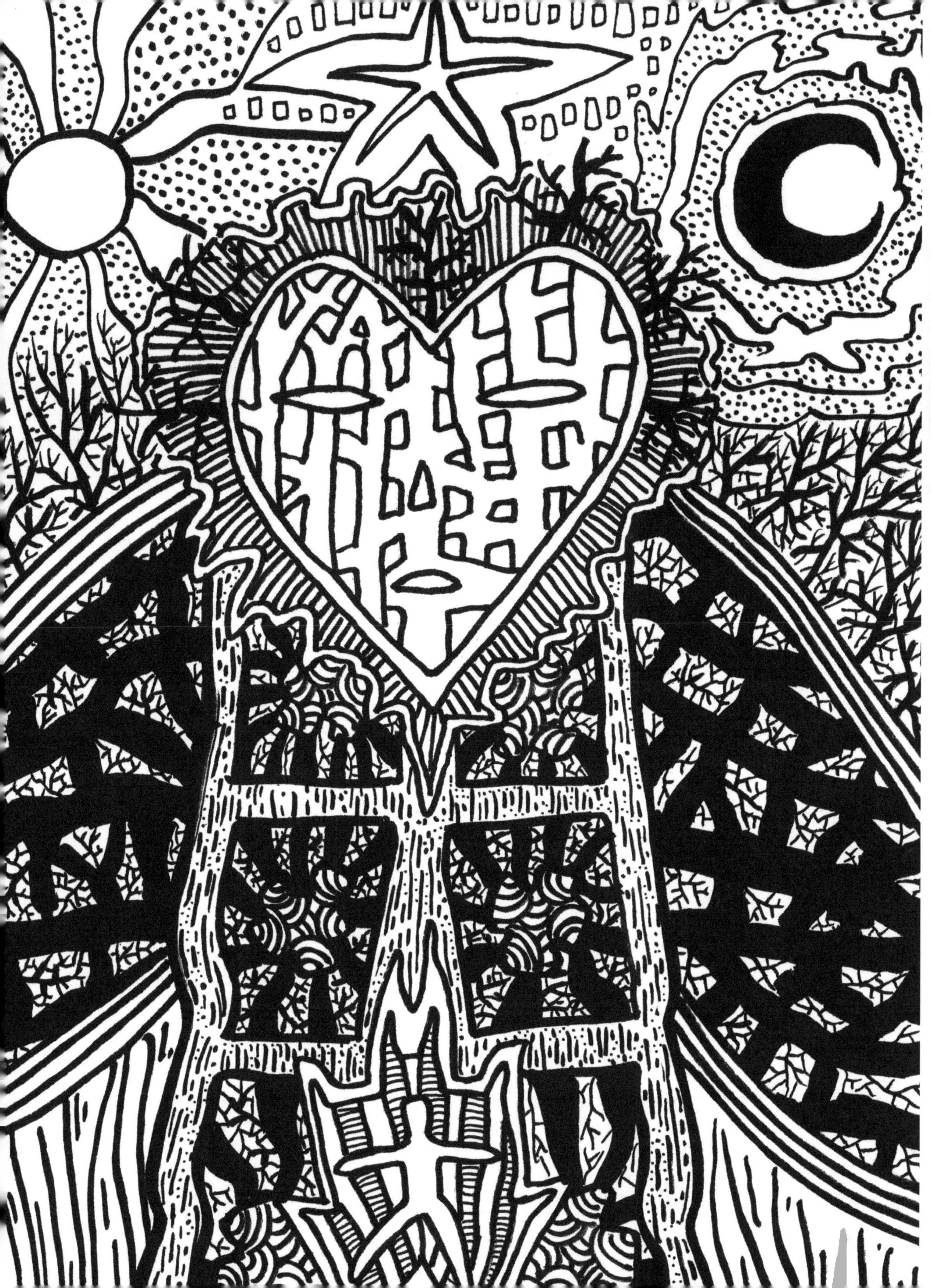

Stove-side conjure bequeathed from stone-age mothers, baby at the breast and sharpened flint in hand to jab at predators. Cookbook grimoire deep in the DNA. Knife cuts clean to the bone. Se kout kouto, se kout pwenyad. Protector of an unbroken chain of life, ushered through the red channels of the birth canal. Howl of labour pain and infant wail. Sleepless nights and double shifts. Battling up the stairwell of her high rise block in pounding rain. Lifting bedraggled pushchair and screaming infant up flights of concrete steps. Opening graf-tagged door onto cramped damp-ridden flat with no heating. Going without a meal to put fish-fingers and chips in small bellies and enough set aside for Christmas.

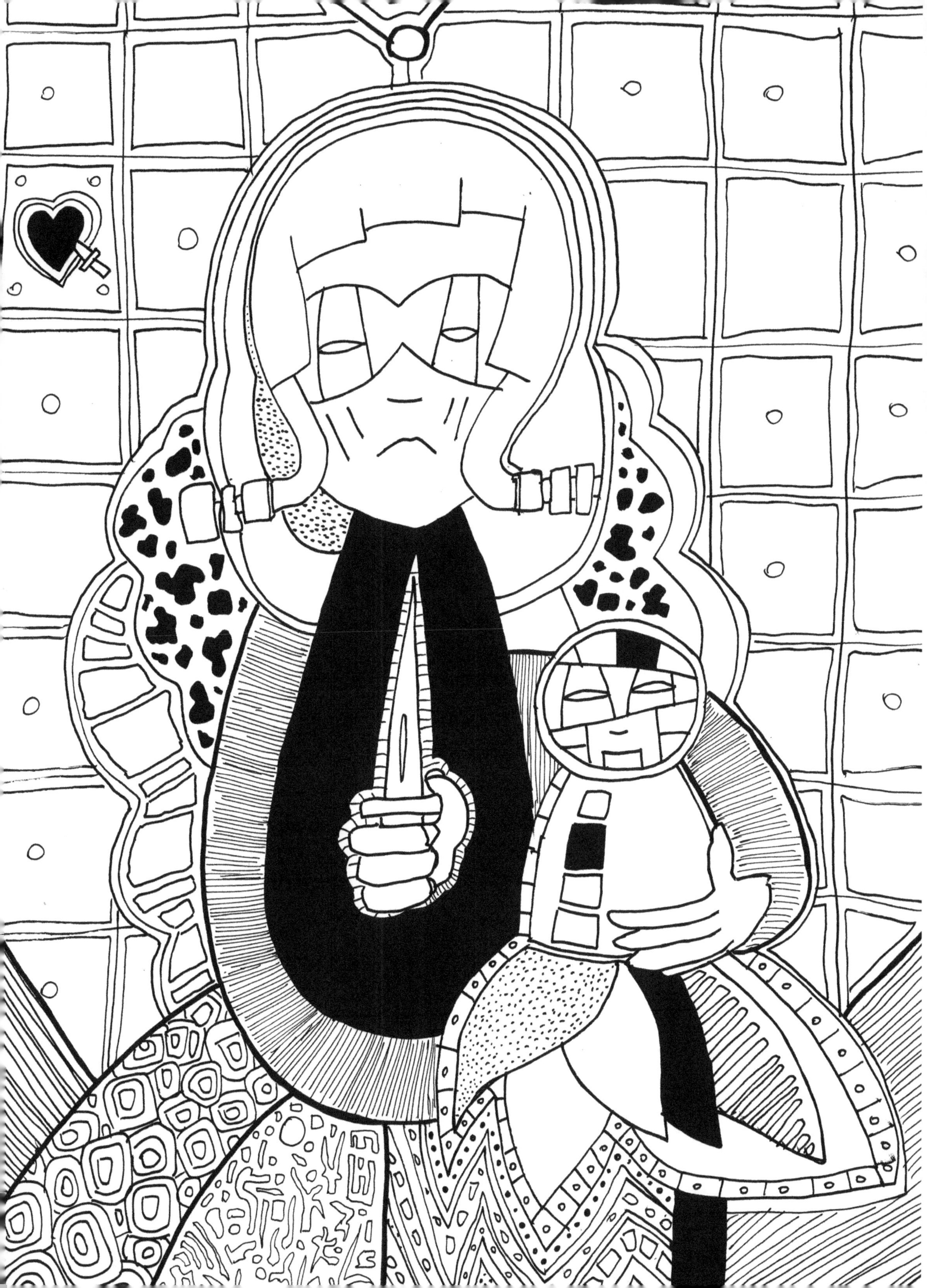

The cowled figure crouches in prayer. Flame of the
Pentecost on the slow burn. The folds of her veil have
become impossible. Where I end and she begins. The split
of her skirt reveals the devil. Brimstone pitchfork and
zig-zag floor. Her face is complex. Her kisses a multitude.
Through a window behind her I can see the primal scene.
She is made of everything yet the truth of her veils itself
in plain sight.

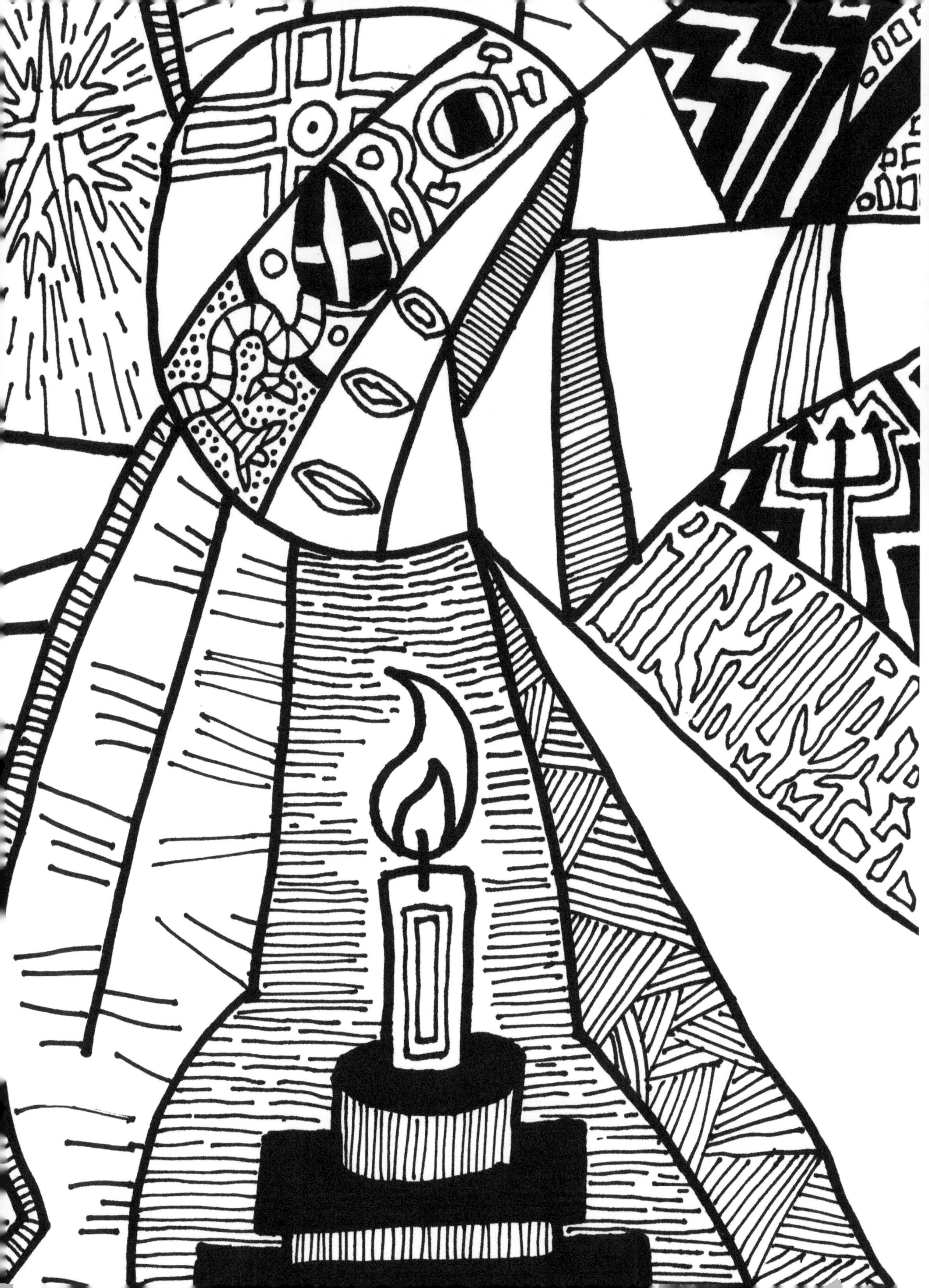

Predators sink roots and seal up windows. Coil deep and
become the fabric. Callused hands steal your faith, hope
and charity. Tent city and detention facility. Red road
to powdered skeleton and confiscated jewellery. Horror
houses policed in neat rows. Skull witness. Hollow vision.
The Angel at your head weeps powerless to intervene in
your betrayal.

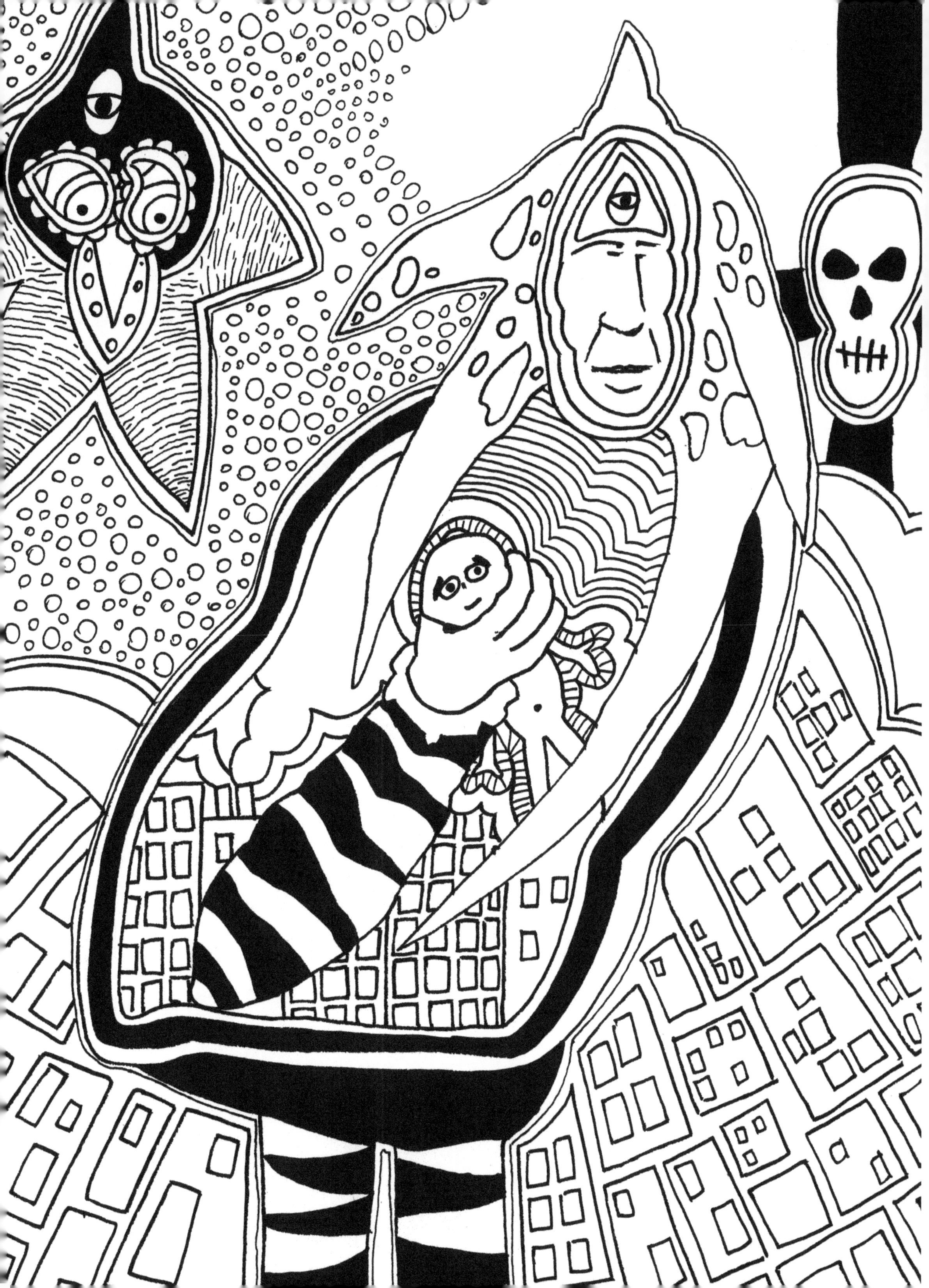

Here comes a candle
to light you to bed
Here comes a chopper
To chop off your head

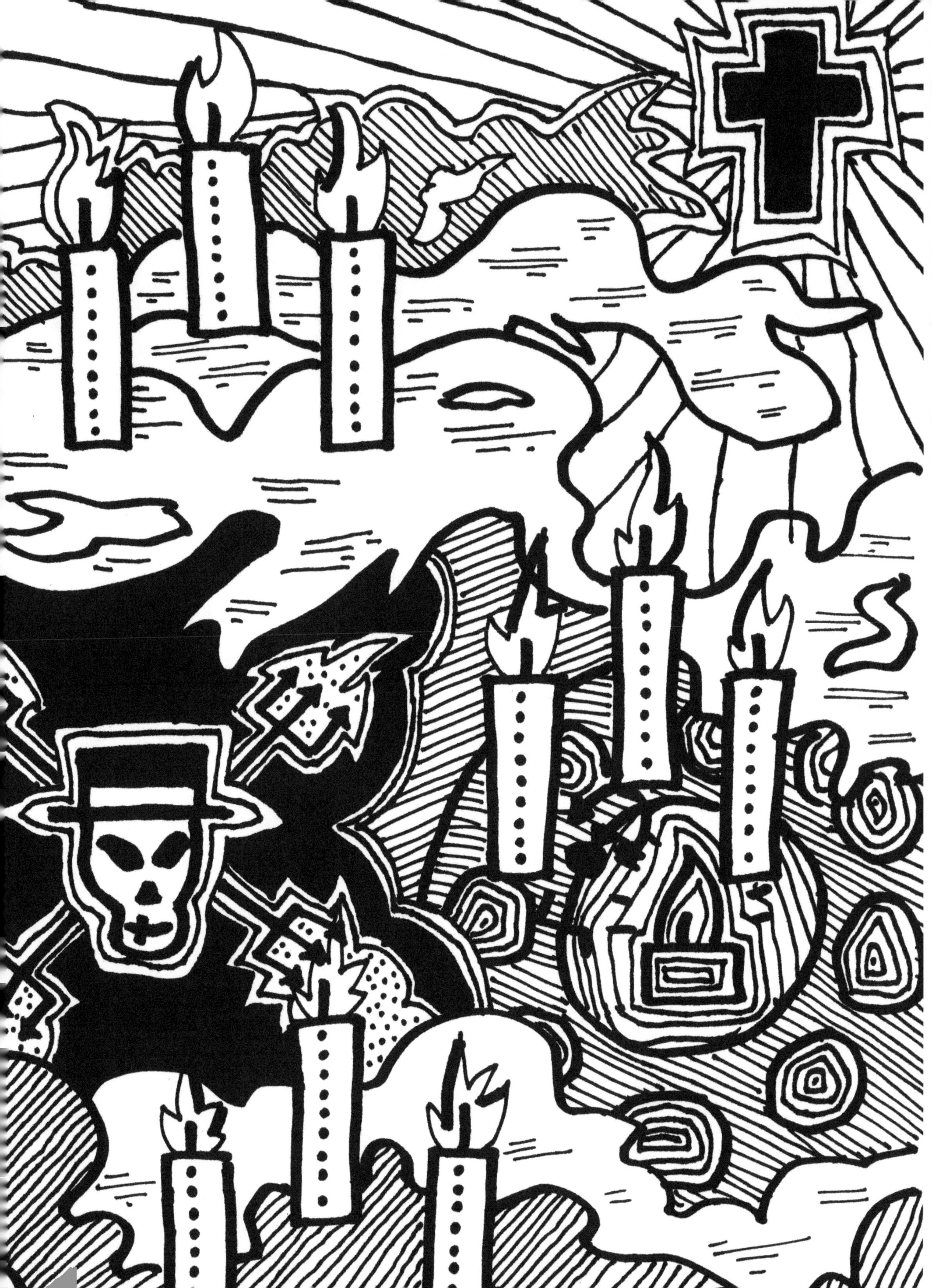

Those that are born to be hanged may fear no drowning.
Calunga buccaneers sail under the Black Flag. Skeleton
within. Grand Upsetter. Man in the Black Hat. Ezekiel
connected dem dry bones. He is all dressed up. He is going
to the palace. Righteous dead on the march. Zombi walk
in broad daylight. Nothing more can be done to them.
Nothing more can be done to you. Set the black lamp.
Tighten the noose. Now hear the word of the Lord.
A message to you Rudy.

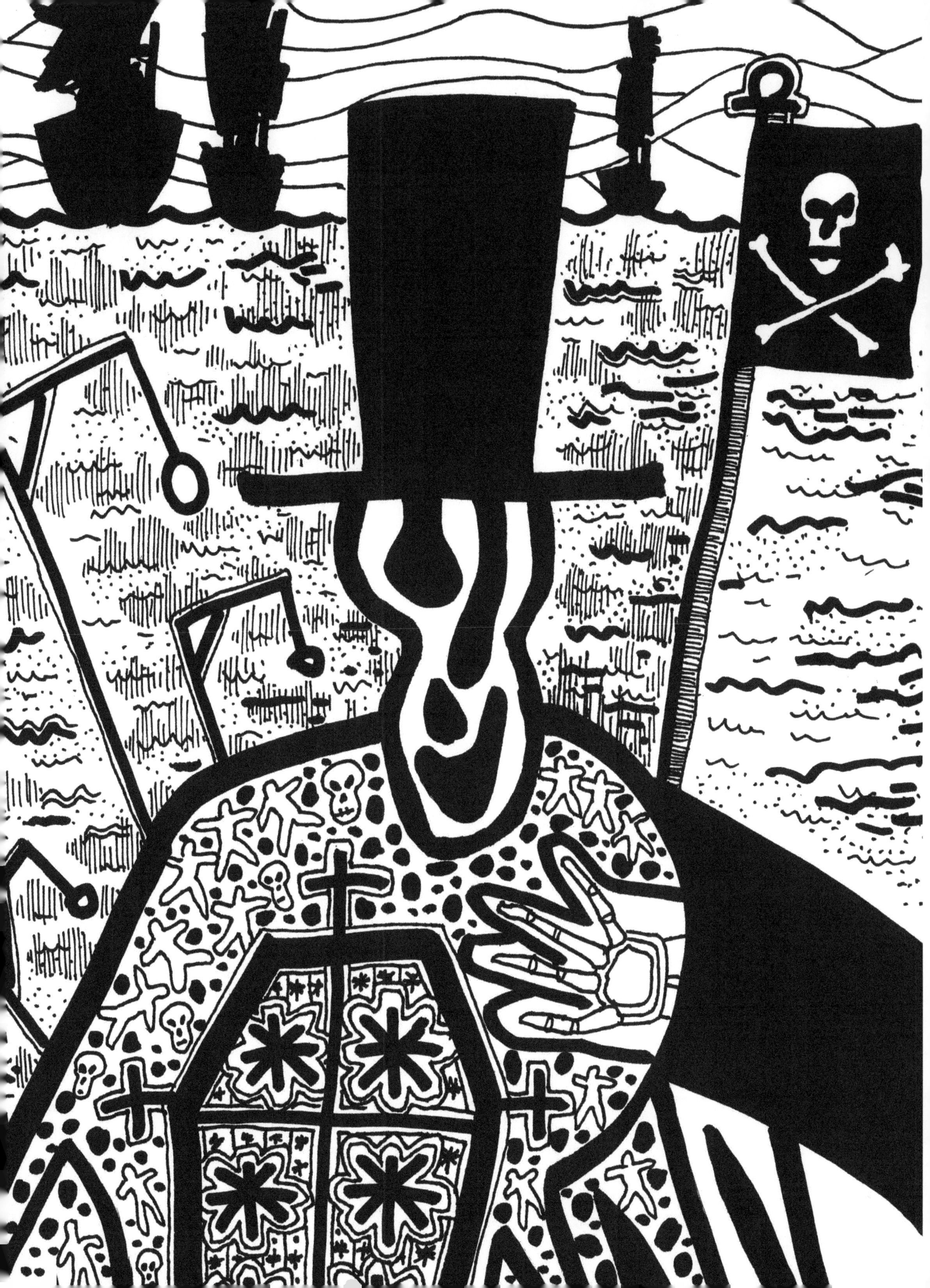

www.ingramcontent.com/pod-product-compliance
Lightning Source LLC
Chambersburg PA
CBHW041050050726
47599CB00018B/2094